BUTTER

Susan Wake

Illustrations by John Yates

Carolrhoda Books, Inc./Minneapolis

#2711

All words that appear in **bold** are
explained in the glossary on page 30.

First published in the U.S. in 1990 by
Carolrhoda Books, Inc.

Library of Congress Cataloging-in-Publication Data

Wake, Susan.
  Butter.

  (Foods we eat)
  Summary: Describes the origin, history, food value,
and uses of butter and examines its use in food prepara-
tion. Includes some recipes.
  1. Butter—Juvenile literature. 2. Margarine—
Juvenile literature. 3. Cookery (Butter)—Juvenile
literature. [1. Butter. 2. Cookery—Butter] I. Title.
II. Series: Foods we eat (Minneapolis, Minn.)
SF263.W35   1990   641.3′72   89-25200
ISBN 0-87614-427-X (lib. bdg.)

Printed in Italy by G. Canale C.S.p.A., Turin
Bound in the United States of America

1 2 3 4 5 6 7 8 9 10 99 98 97 96 95 94 93 92 91 90

Contents

A natural food

Butter has been an important part of our diet for thousands of years. It is made from butterfat, which is a fat that comes from cream. Butter is a natural food product, so artificial flavors, colors, or **preservatives** are not added to it.

There are two main kinds of butter. They are known as sweet cream butter and sour

cream butter. Most butter made in the United States is sweet cream butter. It is made from fresh cream.

Sour cream butter is made by adding special lactic-acid-producing **bacteria** to the cream. The lactic acid that the bacteria produce makes the cream slightly sour and gives the butter a strong taste. Salt may be added to both kinds of butter for flavor and freshness.

The butter we use is made from cows' milk.

Butter in the past

Long ago, people used milk from different animals, such as cows, goats, sheep, and even camels. They soon found that milk turned bad quickly, so they learned how to make other products from it that would keep longer, like yogurt, cheese, and butter.

No one knows when butter was first made. We do know that as long ago as 2000 B.C., people in India made butter from water buffalo's milk. But butter may have been made for the first time by accident.

skimming dish

plunger

wooden iron-bound churn

wooden churn

Perhaps someone carrying milk on horseback found that after the milk had been shaken for a while, little lumps of fat formed in it.

People began making butter by letting milk stand overnight so the cream containing the butterfat could float to the top. At a certain temperature, butterfat forms into granules. The cream containing the butter granules was skimmed off into a churn and shaken, or churned. Churning turns butter granules into butter. The liquid that was left, the buttermilk, was poured off. Then the butter was washed with cold water and kneaded

In the past, special tools were needed for making butter.

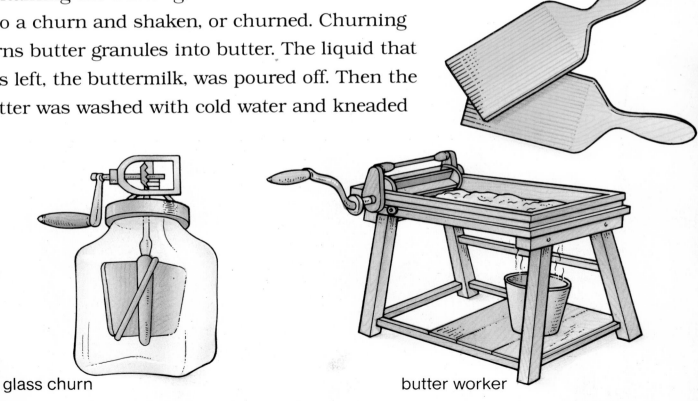

Scotch hands

glass churn

butter worker

to remove air bubbles. Finally the butter was molded into shape.

Many farms used wooden butter molds that had pictures carved inside. The pictures often showed the type of farm the butter had come from. For example a picture of corn cobs meant the butter came from a corn-growing farm. After the butter was molded, it was taken to market to be sold.

The dairy was a cool room where milk was kept,

Butter made on farms was sold at markets. It was cut and weighed in the open air.

Left: These people are making butter in a dairy. The man is using a machine that separates the cream from the milk.

Below: A Bedouin woman in the Middle East is using an animal-skin bag to churn cream.

and where butter and cheese were made. Butter was made mainly by women, called dairymaids.

Sometimes the cream would not churn, so the dairymaids thought witches had cast a spell on it. To counteract the spell, the dairymaids put a red-hot poker into the cream to burn the witches. Chances are the butter didn't churn because it was too cold. The poker raised the temperature and often helped churn the cream to make the butter.

Butter today

The basic way of producing butter is the same today as it was when it was first made. Not many places still use the old method of churning by hand, though. Modern **creameries** use machinery that makes butter in a continuous process. Cream is fed in at one end, and butter comes out at the other.

To collect the cream, milk is heated and fed

The continuous process of butter-making is shown here. After the cream is churned, the butter comes out of the machine in a long strip.

into a high-powered machine called a separator. The separator spins very quickly—about 6,000 times a minute. The cream collects in the middle of the separator because it is lighter than the skim milk, which is flung outward. The cream and skim milk flow out of the separator down different pipes.

If sour cream butter is being made, lactic-acid-producing bacteria are now added. Then the cream for both types of butter is **pasteurized**.

The cream is pasteurized by rapid heating and

Butter is cut into blocks and wrapped by the machine.

11

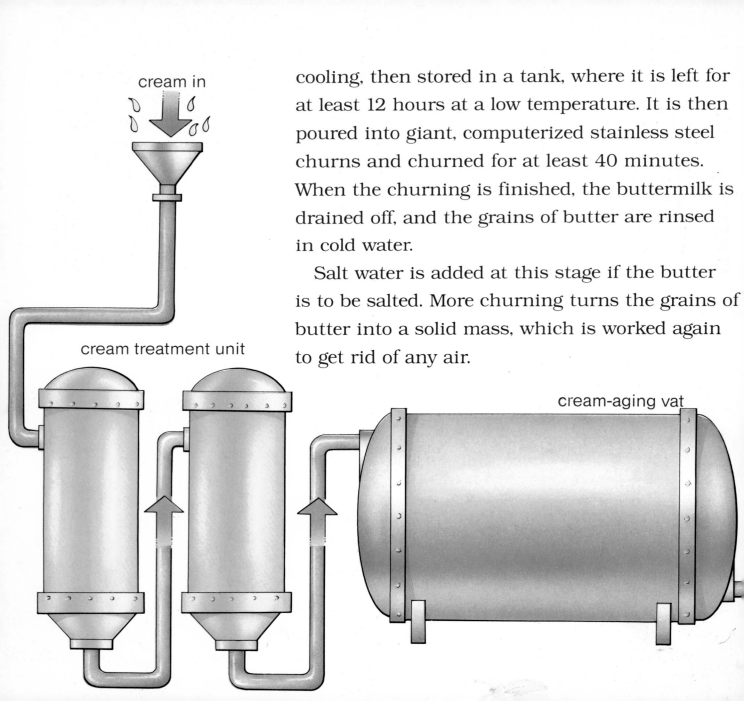

cream in

cream treatment unit

cream-aging vat

cooling, then stored in a tank, where it is left for at least 12 hours at a low temperature. It is then poured into giant, computerized stainless steel churns and churned for at least 40 minutes. When the churning is finished, the buttermilk is drained off, and the grains of butter are rinsed in cold water.

Salt water is added at this stage if the butter is to be salted. More churning turns the grains of butter into a solid mass, which is worked again to get rid of any air.

The butter is formed into a long strip and fed into a packaging machine, where it is cut and wrapped. The packages of butter are weighed, packed into boxes to be delivered to **wholesalers**, and then sent on to stores.

Hygiene is very important in the production process; all equipment must be free from germs. Samples of butter are regularly tested to ensure that they are of the highest quality possible. The packs of butter are stamped with expiration dates, so we can tell when the butter is freshest.

This diagram shows the continuous process of butter-making in a modern creamery.

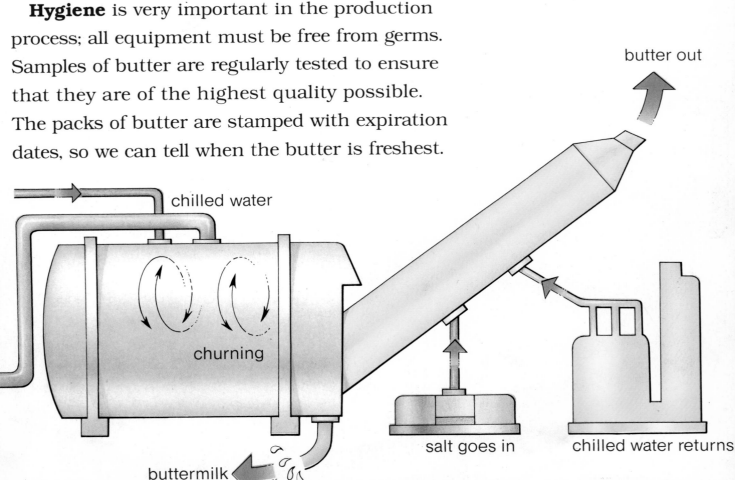

butter out

chilled water

churning

buttermilk

salt goes in

chilled water returns

The food value in butter

Butter contains fat, which our bodies turn into energy. It is also a good source of **vitamins** A and D. Vitamin A is important for good vision, for growth, and for healthy skin. Vitamin D is needed to help build our bones and teeth.

Butter has always been regarded as an important part of our diet, and all dairy products were thought to be good for us. But now

Butter adds flavor to many foods, but eating too much fat can affect your health.

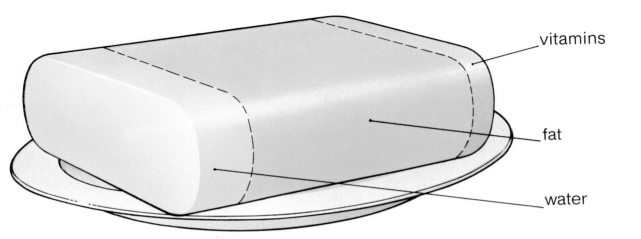

vitamins

fat

water

health experts are not so sure. Rich milk and butter contain a large amount of a substance called **cholesterol**. Too much cholesterol in our diet can clog up our **arteries**, which carry blood from the heart around to other parts of the body. Too much cholesterol can lead to heart disease.

The dairy industry says that the benefits of dairy products in our diet outweigh the possible dangers to our health from cholesterol. People must be careful to choose a balanced diet and to eat a variety of foods.

This diagram shows the different amounts of nutrients in butter.

Make your own butter

It is simple to make your own butter, but it takes quite a lot of shaking, which can make your arms ache, so you may need some friends to help you.

You will need:

A small, clear, screw-top jar, and enough table cream to fill the jar halfway.

1. Wash the jar thoroughly with hot water.

2. Pour in the cream.

3. Screw the top on tightly.

4. Shake, shake, shake...

5. After a while you will notice that the cream separates into a liquid (buttermilk) and into solid grains of butter.

6. Continue to shake until the grains become a solid mass of butter.

7. Pour off the buttermilk and taste the butter that you have made.

You can drink the buttermilk left from your buttermaking.

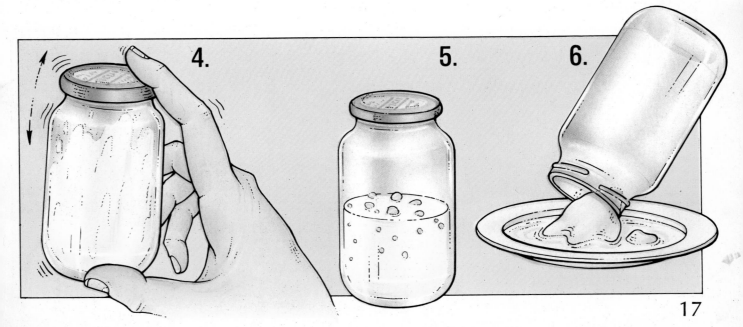

Margarine

In the 1800s, margarine became an important substitute for butter. Many butter factories, like this one in Frankfurt, Germany, were opened.

Margarine was invented in France in the late 1860s. The number of people in France had grown quickly, so more people needed to be fed than ever; butter was becoming scarce. The Emperor Napoleon III

offered a prize to the person who could invent a substitute for butter. A chemist by the name of Hippolyte Mege-Mouries won the prize.

Mege-Mouries made margarine by softening beef fat, which was called *oleo*, and mixing it with salty water, milk, and margaric acid. He called his mixture *oleomargarine*. Margarine was first brought

Margarine is made from oils that are hardened, colored, and flavored. It is formed into blocks to look like butter.

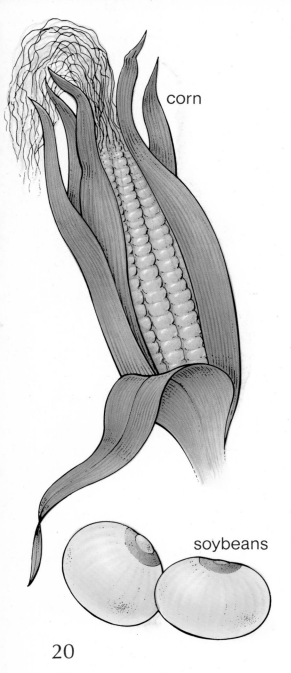
corn

soybeans

to the United States in the early 1870s. It didn't taste very good, and it lacked vitamins, but people were grateful to have any substitute for butter at all. Margarine was cheaper than butter, too.

When beef fat became expensive, the people making margarine had to find other fats to use. They tried various vegetable oils, but oils were too runny. By the early 1900s, however, they found a way to make vegetable oil harder. They also learned how to remove the flavor from oils. Now fats for

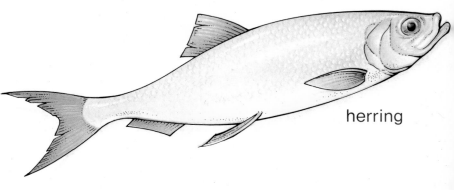
herring

margarine could come from many sources—both plant and animal.

Vitamins were added, so margarine became just as nutritious as butter. Today there are many kinds of margarine. Most margarines have added color, flavorings, and preservatives. Although margarine is required to contain at least 80 percent fat, it has much less cholesterol than butter, and the fat that margarine does have is less harmful than the fat found in butter.

coconut

peanuts

pilchard

sunflower

21

Butter or margarine?

Design a test to see if people can tell the difference between the taste of butter and margarine.

Remember:

Keep the butter and margarine in separate, unmarked containers, and make sure you remember which is which.

Use the same kind of bread or cracker with both butter and margarine.

For the first part of the test, put a little bit of butter and margarine in separate unmarked dishes.

Left: Spread each slice of bread and cracker with either butter or margarine.

Spread equal amounts of butter and margarine on the bread or cracker.

Ask people to try both and tell you which they think is butter and which is margarine.

Write down the results.

What do the results tell you?

If you had to do this test again, what would you do differently?

Ask someone to test you.

Could you tell the difference between butter and margarine?

Below: Can you tell the difference between butter and margarine?

23

Butter in the kitchen

Butter has many uses. It can be eaten as a spread on food like bread, biscuits, scones, or muffins. It is also a basic **ingredient** in many recipes, such as cakes, biscuits, pastry, puddings, and sauces.

Butter can be used to add flavor to vegetables like baked potatoes. It is also often used for frying and grilling. Many people use butter that has been **clarified**. When butter is heated, solids foam to the surface and are skimmed off. The clear, yellow liquid that is left is clarified butter. It is also called ghee.

Butter is usually sold in blocks but can be made into small pats, curls, or cubes.

To keep it fresh, butter should be stored in a cool, dark place away from strong smells. Butter can be frozen, but it will stay fresh in the refrigerator for several weeks. Butter that is going bad will taste and smell very sour.

Butter can be used to make table decorations like this beautiful swan.

Seasoned butters

These are highly seasoned butters that can add flavor to many dishes. Seasoned butters should be well chilled, cut into small pats, and put onto hot food.

Curry butter

You will need:

2 tablespoons butter
1 level teaspoon curry powder
¼ level teaspoon turmeric
1 teaspoon lemon juice

1. Cream the butter until it is soft.

2. Beat in the remaining ingredients.

3. Chill.

26

Garlic butter

You will need:

2 garlic cloves

2 tablespoons butter

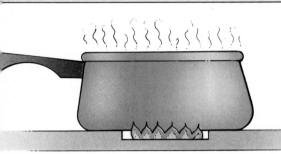

1. Peel the garlic and boil in water for 5 minutes.

2. Drain garlic and chop very finely.

3. Cream the butter until it is soft.

4. Gradually beat in the garlic.

5. Chill.

Bread and butter pudding

You will need, for 4 people:

6 thin slices of bread
2 tablespoons butter
2 tablespoons currants or raisins
2 large eggs
1-2 tablespoons sugar
3 cups milk

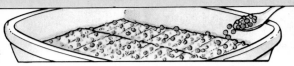

3. Sprinkle with the fruit and half of the sugar.

4. Add the remaining bread, butter side up, and sprinkle with the rest of the sugar.

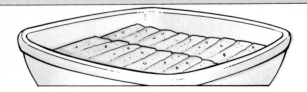

1. Cut the crusts off the bread. Butter the slices of bread.

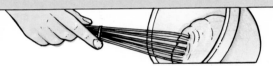

5. Beat the eggs and milk together. Pour over the bread. Let it stand for 30 minutes.

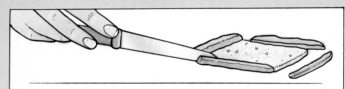

2. Cut the slices into strips and put half of them into a greased 1-quart baking dish.

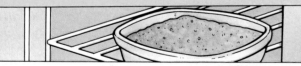

6. Preheat oven to 325° F. Bake in the center of the oven for 45 minutes to 1 hour or until the pudding is set and the top is crisp and golden.

Cheesy biscuits

(makes about 12 biscuits)

You will need:

2 cups flour

⅓ cup butter

3 teaspoons baking powder

1 teaspoon salt

¾ cup milk

¼ cup cheddar cheese

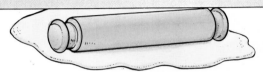

3. Stir the mixture just enough for the ingredients to be combined.

4. Use a rolling pin to roll out the dough so it's about ½-inch thick.

1. Put flour in bowl. Cut in butter.

5. Use a cookie cutter to cut circles into the dough.

2. Add baking powder, salt, milk, and grated cheese.

6. Put the circles on a lightly greased baking sheet. Preheat oven to 450° F and bake for 10 minutes or until brown.

Glossary

arteries: blood vessels carrying blood from the heart through the body

bacteria: tiny living plants that may cause disease. Some may be used to increase the flavor of food, but bacteria can grow rapidly and gradually destroy food.

cholesterol: a fatty substance that is part of all animal tissue. It can coat artery walls, narrowing them and making it hard for blood to pass through.

clarified butter: the liquid that is left after solids have been removed from melted butter

creameries: factories where butter and cheese are made

hygiene: practices, such as cleanliness, that promote health

ingredient: one of the items in a mixture

pasteurized: food that has been heated for a period of time to kill harmful bacteria and prevent spoilage

preservatives: substances added to food to slow the decay of food

vitamins: substances found in small quantities in food that are important to our health

wholesalers: people who buy items in large quantities for the purpose of reselling them to other businesses

Photo acknowledgments

The photographs in this book were provided by: pp. 8, 9 (top), 18, Mary Evans Picture Library; pp. 10, 11, Milk Marketing Board; pp. 9 (bottom), 14, 19, Christine Osborne/ Middle East Pictures; pp. 22, 23, Paul Seheult; p. 25, Topham Picture Library.

31

Index